HARVEST

Other books by Solee MacIsaac
Joy Shared
A Beloved Speck in the Universe
Little Wisdoms
Zen Days, Zen Nights

Harvest

Solee MacIsaac

EVERY BOOK PRESS

MMXXIII

© Copyright 2023 Solee MacIsaac
All rights reserved.
ISBN: 978-0-9837714-8-7

Cover Photo:
Jonathan Parks,
The Bells of Renaissance Vineyard and Winery
Book Design:
William Bentley

INTRODUCTION

There are already enough words here, so I will only add that writing about moments helps me to be present to this one.

Solee MacIsaac

*This small read is dedicated
To my beloved Teacher,
Who inspired all herein.*

Sun, earth, water:
Behold the beautiful
Vineyard of promise.

Vineyard

Following vines to the top of the hill.
They went over and beyond.
I sat down.

The sun sets in the
Vineyard
Like nowhere else.

I saw the bear at a distance,
And he saw me.
He went back to eating port grapes.

Large grape leaves
Make their own shade.
Succulent fruit waits beneath.

In boots and broad brimmed hat,
Fruit flies sticking to damp skin,
My clippers fly from cluster to cluster.

Gathering together
We set out, shivering a little.
Sunrise will come.

If I am very still, spiraling tendrils,
Looking for purchase,
Will wind around my fingertip.

Through the lacy leaf tops,
Sun drops
Glance across my brow.

I can hide here
In the shady
Grape cave.

Listening for the tractor
I rise with the heavy box,
And tip it into the gondola.

Someone is singing,
Heat waves carrying
Uplifting sweetness.

The bells are ringing,
Lunch has arrived,
A final grape pops in my mouth.

It won't be long now,
This section has shed
Its precious bounty.

The slanting shadows
Tell the time left,
'Til the winery-top feast.

Have to wait,
This slope is not
Ripe enough yet.

Aesop's tale is about
Foxes and grapes.
We get bears.

Some of the golden whites
Swinging heavily
Have the botrytis kiss.

Through the gap
I see my friend,
Next row over.

We smile,
And know exactly
How we both feel.

Later,
We share a perfect glass,
Of last year's effort.

Dancing in the moonlight,
Bacchanalian dreams linger,
Between the ravished vines.

High above the striated clouds,
Light beam messages
Descend to ground level in flashes.

Pickers look up,
As highflying geese
Wing across the blazing sky.

Sunlight piercing grape orbs,
Gorgeous and
Indescribable.

I pass others in the rows,
Their hats pulled down,
Conserving strength and sight.

It seems we are all one,
The aim for each
Shared by the others.

Joyous night revels,
Wine kegs,
Music and laughter.

Hearts aligned
For another day ahead
Of garnered ruby clusters.

Love, work, sharing,
Friendship, respect,
And gratitude abound.

We seem to be a particle
Of something immense
And significant to nature.

Wandering through
The emptied vines
Is both sad and satisfying.

Someone walks by
With a fan built into his hat.
We each cope in our own way.

The slopes shimmer
In the September heat,
Afternoon meltdown.

Planting, pruning, tying,
Seasonal work continues,
The reward is harvest.

Watching the tractor climb
To the winery,
Precious cargo to deliver.

Deep purples, reds, golds;
Magnificent fruit
At the peak of perfection.

Diving back into leafy shelter,
More babes to deliver
With my purple-stained hands.

Surrounding mountains
Witness this celebration
Of the grape.

I listen to the clippers near me,
Dedicated work;
This moment forever mine.

Monks work, repetitive,
Contemplative, refining
Each fragment of earth to soul.

An unexpected downpour
Of blessed relief
Cleanses salty brows.

Raindrops enhancing
Jeweled orbs,
Even more enticing than before.

Vineyards, like hearts
And music,
Have a singular beat.

Harvest was a bright spark
In the heart of the jewel
Of our School.

Slow work,
The celebration
Of grapes to liquid magic.

But suddenly
The vines are bare
And we are done.

Weather watching,
Rain can make grapes too fleshy,
The first drop is large and splashes.

Halting harvest is a big deal,
But necessary,
Ensuring quality is key.

To move together in the heat of day
To the next shining slope,
Is glorious.

A curious wren
Perches atop my vine;
Raising my visor to see, he flees.

Ants find my boot interesting.
Resting in grape shade,
I sip my coffee.

Regular life continues,
This bubble is a step aside;
Reaping memory along with fruit.

The quiet effort
Each student makes
Glistens in the heart of our vineyard.

The good produced
Is far more
Than the next bottle on the shelf.

Someone's dog is nuzzling my elbow,
I turn to a face-licking pile of fur
And stumble into my grape box.

Sudden wind sweeps through,
Scattering dry leaves and dust.
A moment to refocus on intent.

We are soldiers of the grape:
Our armor, only clippers;
Our shield, our Presence.

Love guides us through days,
Nights are filled with after-images,
Those picked, to pick, and right here.

Loving hands salute
Across the rows
With full hearts beaming.

Distillation to come,
Winery filled with robust fruit,
Many hands reach to the task.

Cold water is passed around,
Refreshing throats and minds,
Things as they are, myself as I am.

The infinite blue of the Summer sky
Rises endlessly above
The simmering grape world below.

Seeing the rocky earth,
Sprouting vines, heavy with grapes,
Gnarled and empty, all at once.

In a moment, timeless
And containing all time,
I breathe.

The only perfection
Is letting all
Fly to Heaven.

Within and without
There is:
Grand Harvest.

We celebrate a task completed
To honor efforts made
And acknowledge our part in it.

Dropping all pretenses,
Essence forward,
Smiling in the long heated pathway.

Through repetitive work,
Imagination crawls back again.
Best to stay alert.

Each step, each clip, each breath;
Eyes open and seeing,
Forward progress happens.

Winding around the hill
Sloping to the south,
Deer are having lunch in the vines.

Near the orchard now,
Delicious fragrance wafting
Toward the hungry pickers.

Break-time poetry
Lifts our inner life
To the brim of state change.

A good friend
Massages my tired neck muscles,
A sunrise in my inner world opens.

An accident occurs,
The tractor gets stuck in a trench,
Many friends shoulder the retrieval.

The interruption
Isn't, really.
We continue, because we must.

Hearts are open,
Deep sharing
Happens beneath the vines.

Students in the kitchen,
Baking, cooking, preparing
Our sustenance.

Students driving to town
For groceries, supplies;
We who serve, are served.

Flying through the shimmering air
Positive energy
Supports continuing efforts.

Most of the red wine flavor
Comes from the dark rich skins;
Stains visible on vineyard clothes.

Heavy white clouds block sunlight,
Spreading a hint of coolness;
Temporary illusion.

Our sustenance depends
On many past seekers
Who have broken the rocky ground.

There is so much to be grateful for,
To waste a moment in trivial pursuit
Seems beyond wasteful.

What was before, what will be,
All is now:
Laid out in grand array.

From earth to grape
Woody trunk links
Sky and ground together.

Why here? Why now?
This passage of time,
Has meaning from above.

One more drop of ruby goodness
Savoring life and art,
With the toss of the glass.

Earth gives up her secrets
To the grape,
As do we – transformed by wine.

Living here, loving here,
Earth, sun, healthy growing vines,
Being here – best, like nowhere else.

Grapes cascade into the gondola
From all sides,
An indigo waterfall.

Are we caretakers of the grape?
Or is the vineyard
Our haven of re-education?

Bubble gum clouds,
Hover over emerald mountain,
Crystal blue lake reflecting all.

Vineyard stretching to the horizon,
Geometric rows ending in roses,
Leafy wonders hiding purple secrets.

What is bigger than God?
What is smaller than God?
Same answer: Nothing.

The microcosm: vineyard
Holds all phases of grapevine life,
We are the moving aspect.

We are water-filled like grapes,
We ripen in our lives,
Who is there to harvest us?

The only way to love the
Questions,
Is to be the answer.

Weary after revels
Creaky bones crave rest,
Vine visions interrupt deep sleep.

New morning, waking before birds,
Can't wait for breakfast;
Sunrise slanting over vines.

A blaze of light
Domes the sky,
Lightning flash shocks senses.

A dragonfly zips by my vision,
Reminding me to stay here,
Where and when, I am.

A jet thunders overhead
Disturbing peaceful silence,
Modern world vs. Ancient activity.

Bouncing energy of the morning
Turned to heavy steps
At dusk.

A warm feeling of completion
Circulates with the cooler breeze,
Time to hang up clippers and gloves.

Nature's seasonal cycle
Reflects our inner phases,
We are natural and supernatural.

Hummingbird visits
My flower-patterned brim,
Not good enough for him.

Seems this vine overproduced…
My box is full again.
An empty one is thrust under my feet.

Gentle murmurs of students
Conversing invisibly
Tickle my ears.

Love is shown in so many ways.
We are Love-drenched,
And grateful.

Children ever perceptive
Dance with happiness
Between the vine rows.

Many events throughout the year
Bring joy and special efforts,
Harvest has its own drama.

It is a particular treat
To remember harvest
From the year on the label.

Vintage – my year,
Robust, fruity,
Good nose and lots of legs.

Deep blue sky
Infinitely ascends above
We who follow the vines to their end.

Coyotes howling in the distance,
Moonrise near the horizon,
One more row before I rest.

My neighboring picker hands me
A lemon drop,
A shade-checkered smile on his face.

We lovers of the grape,
Live, love, and laugh
Together.

Paying close attention
To the regular clipping actions,
Internally and externally.

The work is done for the day.
Though tired
I wander through the moonlit rows.

Gentle laughter around the table,
Good wine, good friends,
Celebrating our shared efforts.

A bonfire sends sparks heavenward,
Reminding of the inner spark
To keep ignited.

Too tired to hold hands
We trudge homeward,
Fatigued but deeply satisfied.

So close, the heat, the sun,
The very smells and sounds;
Between here and here, I am.

When a friend gains,
We all miraculously
Gain.

Letting go of fear and pain
Leaves an amazing
Space.

A second birth
With eye wide open
Is the miraculous.

Grapes feed us
To be food for the gods,
The ultimate privilege.

Breaktime, fresh hot muffins
Are passed around,
Rest and treats, much appreciated.

A sprinkle of raindrops
Enough to bring forth
A spectacular rainbow.

Although conversations happen,
Mostly the vineyard is quiet:
Sweet silence.

Love and nature
Don't need worshippers,
Only life and lovers.

A grand venture:
Grape growing, winemaking,
Being creating.

Loving the moment
Seeing ourselves seeing,
Treasures beyond measure.

Have we been planted, grown roots,
Limbs reaching, bearing fruit?
Will we be distilled, becoming what?

Bouquet of colorful
Grape leaves adorn my hair,
Like Circe I whirl in the Autumn sun.

Light overhead filling
Heart, mind, body,
Soul enlightened.

Sun drenched,
Star drenched,
Love drenched.

Singing around the fireplace,
Mugs of chocolate and
Good feelings exchanged.

Bright promise
Of new loves,
Friends become closer.

Sharing all we are
In the highest sense
Renews the capacity to grow.

The venue for our Play
Is wherever we are,
Whatever we are doing.

A vineyard
Is a good place
To grow a soul.

The clamoring internal voices
In a single moment
Are shut out in beatific silence.

Lightning strikes sometimes,
But not a source
For regular fuel.

Momentary efforts
Add up to daily, weekly, yearly
Understandings without words.

Red, gold, amber leaves curl
Around my boot
And crunch in the pathway.

It is quiet on this slope,
The others have slipped away
Leaving me to finish my song.

The start of the day
In the first light rays
Presents rosy promise of completion.

Sitting down to the long table feast
Friends crowd around
To toast the new vintage unbottled.

The past and the future
Are part of our present
And reside together in eternity.

Climbing the stairway
To the starry heavens
Is a moment-by-moment endeavor.

Transforming the ails of the day,
The groans of the night;
Plus all difficulties, is the pathway.

Hang the lanterns and pennants,
Blow up the balloons,
Celebrate our ultimate success.

Bending, kneeling, squatting,
Close to the earth,
Inhaling the very air of grape vines.

Lavish cloud layers
Pile and build sky mountains,
Harboring Autumn rainstorms.

There is nothing to fear,
We trust and rely on each other,
To do the divine work of ages.

Charged with the finest energy
We can acquire,
We move upward into the Light.

Simple, quiet, light,
Work is joy
In this state.

Distant haze on the mountain
Paints vineyard rows
With Easter egg hues.

Blood, fire, molten rock,
Jolting electricity, cracks in earth:
Nothing compares to World 6.

Up at the winery mysterious
Alchemy transports grape juice:
White to tanks, red to barrels.

The graceful lady
Wafting through our labor
Brings pure beauty to each brow.

Though we are not stomping
On grapes with bare feet,
Our tangible connection is strong.

Stretching out under a tree,
Listening to the murmur of students
Conversing, resting in the shade.

The Teacher walks the rows,
A trail of joy in his wake,
Each of us grateful in our hearts.

A powerful dream
Creates new fervor
To experience every moment.

A pristine glass of new wine,
Held to the light,
Toasts the season's pinnacle.

There is so much to love
In the timeless world
Of Uncreated Light.

The many lifetimes
Might suffer
The lack of a vineyard.

The center of the rose
Has a secret
Revealed only to a nose.

A bee covets the cluster
In my gloved hand,
Watching her flight entrances.

Butterflies, bees, dragonflies
See all from above;
As can we, in the right state.

Midday heat, though oppressive,
Is the medium through which
We learn to swim.

The turning of the Earth
Brings a new day
To begin again the infinite reality.

Palm tree beings
Bend and sway
In the changing weather.

One more box to fill to the brim
With nature's gifts,
Then I will sink to the deep shade.

A hand on my shoulder,
A lift by my elbow,
A friend helps me on my way.

We could not do this alone;
Outside help is greatly needed
And graciously provided.

As much as we want to be true,
Deceptions worm their way back,
When we aren't looking.

Sometimes it is difficult
To accept worthiness
For the bounteous Harvest.

Bowing low with clasped hands,
Deep in gratitude
For our very excellent fortune.

Riding the love flow
Into the heart of harvest
We celebrate the gods' gifts.

Rattles alert my instinctive senses,
A slithering crosses my path,
A sudden boot slams down hard.

A hawk lands on the vine post
Fifty yards ahead;
He screeches taking flight.

The natural world
Is simple in its complexity,
A good example to follow.

Images fall upon my eyes
Like snowflakes in Winter,
Encompassing early Autumn beauty.

Living in the moment
Pulls the ends together,
Past and future into eternity.

The pickers dance
From vine to vine
Swirling to the music of the spheres.

What angel designed
This magnificent vine,
Heavy with generous globes of life?

So many hearts singing
In unison,
Harmony of Heaven.

Born to breathe a specific number
Of times, a specific number of lives,
Until rebirth into a higher world.

Down the slope to the pond,
To rinse my handkerchief,
I spot the large bushy tail of a fox.

An unusual breeze lifts my hair
And raises my brows,
I hear a whisper.

Extra care climbing back to my row,
No one is around;
Being alone is a pleasant illusion.

In the depths of Summer,
Moisture bereft,
The pond looks mighty enticing.

Some students can resist no longer,
Shed garments and
Splash into cool relief.

The tractor rumbles by
With a trail of vineyard pickers
Smiling and fanning each other.

The goodness in this endeavor
Outstandingly clear
And jubilant.

Hail the sweet grapes,
Soon to become
Divine nectar for all.

Vineyard is reflected in your eyes,
Can you see the love in mine?
It fills me to eye level and spills out.

Tipsy from wine
We share a song
Not always on key.

At the hilltop
The view invites
Wonder and expansion.

Lunch at the observatory
A special treat,
Viewing vineyard from above.

At the bonfire, sipping wine,
Watching sparks
Fly to the stars.

Heat in the Summer:
Sometimes difficult;
Heat in the Winter: lifesaving.

The empty vines
Could be sad,
But really, they are relieved.

Moonrise over the vineyard,
Reflected light
Of our beautiful star.

Seen from above
The vineyard hill pattern
Is stripes and rings.

I saw a cat that wasn't there
A second later,
Or the one before.

Refining the moment,
Perfect cluster, perfect clip,
Presence experienced through eye.

Liquid grapes, distilled, refined,
Transformed
Into holy wine.

Walking slower now,
Heat pulling at my heels,
Many thoughts go sliding by.

Each step serves a purpose,
Each moment collected,
Makes a life.

Sitting in a circle
On crumbly leaves
The flames reflected on rosy faces.

Bonfires, moonlight,
Stars and sun,
Forever memory cues of harvest.

Have I been changed by harvesting?
A connection has been forged
Between below and above.

Dancing, singing, laughing,
The celebration of the grape
Is a nightly privilege.

Toast to the magical moment,
When grape juice
Becomes delicious wine.

Sky fills with sooty clouds,
Breathing difficult,
Fire – close to vineyard!

Days of smoke,
Craving blue sky,
Grateful vineyard is safe.

Don't get me wrong, it is tough stuff,
Bending, squatting, heat, flies,
Sore muscles, but lovely grapes.

My solace for Monk's work
Humbly performed:
Inner quiet.

Seeing how integral
Vineyard and pickers,
Eternal process teaches wholeness.

Watching the dipping, twisting,
Yellow kite, against the bluest sky,
Wondering who is flying it.

Shining encompassing light
Above and in my head
Reveals the meaningful world.

Mistakes happen,
We learn,
Watching inside and out.

Following the love path
Eyes and hearts full,
Minds empty and spacious.

The winery looms ahead,
Providing generous shade,
Up the hill, lined with cypress.

Someone passes with a babe
Papoose style,
Sleeping peacefully.

Looking up through the leaves
I see a smiling face,
Love circulates freely in the vineyard.

If you love something
You take care of it;
In eternity, it is yours.

Like love, valuation
Is not really taught,
Only gifted.

The twisted vines
Struggle in the rocky soil,
And produce excellent flavors.

The science of the grapes,
Readiness for picking,
Is complex and necessary.

How much more so
Our suitability
For higher possibilities.

Hand to hand,
Heart to heart,
The work proceeds.

Geese flying south already,
Reminding of season change,
And the coolness of Autumn.

Inner courage is required
To persist in any lengthy endeavor:
Will, love, and presence.

Although they are faint,
I can hear the bells chiming,
Even at the far edge of the vineyard.

With arms around
Each other's shoulders,
We proudly sing the day's ending.

The vines eat the air, the sun,
And the earth.
Then produce flowers and fruit.

Our bodies do something similar,
But what of our souls?
What do they eat and produce?

The inner light domed and
Ever present,
Opens the doors of clarity.

Without help
From outside sources,
All is lost.

All it takes is:
Enlightened attention,
A helping hand, and luck.

Heading toward the small tree grove
I pass some grape-stained friends,
Throwing fruit and laughing together.

Grape vine,
Fine wine,
Mellow time – Allons-y!

A wreath of grape leaves in my hair,
Dancing, spinning before the pyre.
A spell of transformation on my lips.

Bewitched by magic,
You drink my potion,
The ruby kiss of wine.

Wild days of revelry,
All negative energies eliminated,
Nothing remains of myself.

Work, play, hill climbing,
Sun, breeze, nature,
All whirls around and penetrates.

"Hello," someone I have never met;
A smiling face kisses my cheek,
New student, new picker.

Almost as if another's hands
Are moving mine,
From vine to vine.

A swamper comes by
And captures my full box,
Behold! It's my son!

Whoops! A friend clipped her hand,
First aid to the rescue,
The tractor driver supplies.

Sweet breeze lifts my hair
And tickles my neck,
Strength is replenished.

Being responsible to this moment
I take it in deeply,
And watch inside and out.

Wayward grape bounces off my hat,
Looking up,
I spot the culprit.

Grape wars are not so uncommon,
Small distraction,
In a long undertaking.

Flirtations happen,
Essence dominates,
Undercurrent is divine love.

A wink, a smile, a kiss,
An arm around a waist,
Affectionate workers beam.

It is so simple
To be in this moment,
Just let go of all unreal.

Come join the party,
There is space and time
For you to Be.

The vineyard
Is a lovely place
To fill senses with presence.

Empty your cup,
Fill it up with new wine,
Blessed by the harvest of love.

Whirring opaline wings,
Dragonflies low,
Above the mountain pond.

Following the row around the hill
I spot my group of pickers
Sitting down to break.

Greeting friends with tired smiles
The satisfied glow of arrival
On their faces.

Trading shoulder rubs,
Sharing treats,
Students take care of each other.

It is too hot now for the white grapes;
We move to the Cabernet slope,
Our afternoon laid out before us.

Carefully we tip our full boxes
Of very ripe grapes into the bins,
They must not be crushed yet.

The purple fairies drop their
Magic dust over harvested fruit,
Preserving perfect form.

A wild flower patch
Waves lightly in the breeze,
Gently we pluck them for our hair.

Making poems in our heads,
We giggle and tell them
To each other.

Delirious in heat and love,
Laughter is prevalent
Swimming in sunlight.

The artistry of the terraced vineyard
A continuous visual impression
Affecting all functions.

We are at the top of the mountain,
Love-immersed view fills our senses,
Mountains surround miles of vines.

Grateful for our Play,
We sing and dance
To inner music.

Limited time to bring in all the reds
Before the sugars are too high.
We pick up our pace.

Aspiring to the highest state,
Being home wherever we are,
Each breath a chance to begin.

Love isn't something we do,
It is the medium
In which we thrive.

Looking at my hands,
Wondering at the mystery of life,
Students are unique and the same.

Soaking up the sunlight
I turn my face to the sky just in time
To watch a red-tailed hawk zoom by.

Birds of prey on their job,
Catching small creatures,
Nature's cycle of life.

The highest beings
Use the lightest energies
To fuel their existence.

The blood of the earth
Rises up into the vines,
Becoming beautiful grape juice.

Each part of the process
Gives a new perspective
On the whole immense work.

Some pickers manage to look fresh;
I am not one,
The sun has taken its toll on me.

Time, that elastic dimension,
Has tricked me again.
But here I am, now, once more.

Stunning how quickly things flow
To their source
When the day is done.

The half-heard sounds
Of students trekking back
To their cars is almost sad.

A few half-filled boxes are making
Their way to the tractor,
While I mop my brow.

Surveying the empty vines,
It all seemed so fast,
Even though the moments were long.

Beginnings and endings
Seem wrapped up together,
In this genuine reality.

Her eyes are watering;
It's the dust, she stammers.
I understand.

Mostly done, except for port grapes,
Stragglers gather
To celebrate the amazing haul.

Bins are stacked on the flatbed
For the one-way trip up
The mountainside.

The mysterious winery on the hill
Where all grape clusters
Migrate to their fate.

Many students await the final grapes
Embracing all we have delivered,
To begin the next phase.

Winery

Giant concrete building,
Dug into the top of the hill,
Shelters tanks, barrels, and students.

The space inside is as big
As outside,
Space is inside out.

Stone-like, echo-y, high ceilings;
Winery,
Cool and inviting after Summer heat.

Top floor, tanks, lab and offices;
Second floor, maintenance;
Level one, barrels, bottling, labeling.

Some say the winery is
Dank and gloomy,
Harvest makes it bright with activity.

So many grapes crowding into
The coolness,
So begins the transformation.

We don't even have the capacity
To understand
How lucky we are.

Excitement circulates
From students to
Their winemaking machinery.

Time doesn't really exist,
But our experience
Of it does.

The elasticity of time
Can be
Deceptive.

Timing is essential
In good winemaking.
As in soul creating.

The crane moves a bin of whites
To the top of the
Crusher/destemmer.

Juice drains out,
Skins are moved to
An inflatable bladder.

Intense squeezing
Removes the last
Trickle of white grape juice.

Stainless steel tank
Is the new home
For pearly golden nectar.

Samples go to the lab,
Many alternative decisions
Considered.

Seeds, stems removed from reds,
Skins stay with ruby juice,
Fermentation happens in the tank.

When it's ready,
New red wine is moved
To barrels for oaky flavor.

Topping up each barrel,
Necessary over time,
As evaporation occurs in dry air.

Winemaking,
A scientific attempt
To entice spirits to the party.

While vineyard pickers
Are soaking in tubs,
Winery workers are busy as bees.

All-important sugar levels
Checked and rechecked,
Grapes self-create wine.

Tubes carry wine to different
Winery levels,
Bloodstream of the building.

Roof of the winery,
Called the "lid,"
Where celebrations are held.

Elements, physics, concentration,
Aspects of producing fine wine,
But especially, alchemy.

Large spaces,
Large machines,
Aroma of wine pervades.

A student passes me a frothing
Glass of new wine;
My head spins, alcohol very high.

Tanks are doing their job,
Time for fun,
We hold a Halloween Party.

After bottling
We run labels
Through the glue machine.

Hand-positioning each label
On every bottle,
Then burnishing it in place.

Bottles are boxed and ready
For storage –
"Fete" accompli!

Working together,
Feeling pride in accomplishment,
Always with an eye to higher world.

Special sale!
Wine tasters crowd together,
Anticipating the next treat.

Botrytis-infected raisins
Have made wonderful
Late harvest dessert.

Red wine is my medicine,
Raise a glass
To health and well-being for all.

Inside the winery,
Seems a bit somber,
Compared to the sun frenzy outside.

There is a smooth energy
Of movement to a focused
Completion of perfect product.

Each student responsible
For their own inner life;
Light shining from their faces.

Open to learning,
Happy to labor for the whole,
Work ethic in place, serving highest.

Distillation occurring
Inside and out,
The motions proceed.

Harvest party is brewing,
Many hands cook and decorate,
Preparing the musical feast of wine.

Sunrise over the mountain,
Students enter the winery levels,
Each having their assigned duties.

Awareness of awareness
Grows in
Inner silence.

We share the same
Inner space,
Of pure shining emptiness.

A brief glance,
A subtle smile,
Reminding each other to stay awake.

Finest energies of our efforts
Collect and radiate
From our hearts.

Bottlers and packers
Hum along to an unknown tune,
Each octave moves at its own pace.

The result: sumptuous wine
To savor and applaud,
A celebration of the vine.

Within and without
The medium of the grape,
Produces conscious students.

Driving down slope,
Past the pond and Theatron,
We park and walk to lunch.

Light from the higher world
Shines just as evenly in the Winery,
As it does in the Vineyard.

It takes conviction
To create a vineyard and winery,
And a lot of help.

Many efforts and time
Are necessary
For the richest Cabernet Sauvignon.

Few experts, but many
Attentive students,
Learn the art of creating finest wine.

On the lid singing songs
Under the stars,
Setting the stage for tomorrow.

Diving into the work
Once again,
With renewed efforts.

The depths of the winery
Is a good place
To practice inner silence.

Reminders are needed,
As well as help from above:
Singularity, another illusion.

A friend hands me a glass
Of Chardonnay,
Golden wine from white clusters.

My favorite, Sauvignon Blanc,
Isn't quite ready,
Very much worth waiting for.

Varietals are sometimes mixed,
Blends can create surprising flavors,
The lab winemakers excel.

Syrah, Merlot, Zinfandel,
Beautiful red wines, bottled,
Corked, labeled, and ready to taste.

Visitors love our wines;
Hosting a tasting
Is a joy to watch faces alight.

Oddly, they are as curious
About us,
As they are about our wines.

We are closer than ever,
Inner space and outer space
Have converged.

One kiss,
Beauty, harmony, inner peace
Expand to the edges of our Selves.

Love, like our Selves,
Is difficult to explain,
But we know it when we feel it.

Growing up in the midst of focused
Efforts toward a common aim,
Is maturing our deepest levels.

The alchemy of the moment
Is winemaking;
On a higher level, it is soul-making.

Grieving a friend's loss,
All are touched deeply,
By the seriousness of life.

The work must continue,
With open hearts
And shared remembrances.

Walking through the empty rows,
We chat on the way to lunch,
Another group replaces us.

When all is barreled, tanked,
Bottled, boxed,
We enjoy our own wine together.

It is a grand concept
To create a vineyard and winery,
To create our Selves much grander.

First eye sees patterns,
Second eye sees depth,
Third eye sees truth.

There are worlds within worlds,
Size, dimension, time, density –
Really, there is only: here, now.

It can be confusing
Without the clear light of
Presence.

No matter the weather,
The winery keeps
Cool and even temperature.

Wine bottles and barrels
Need constant temperature
To preserve goodness.

Students also are kept from
Harmful extremes
By divine benefactors.

We grow and learn through
The Play assigned to each;
Real work is always before us.

Even when we create light,
The light we didn't create,
Creates us.

Although destiny
Is difficult to determine,
Fate is secure in present moment.

Standing in divine light,
Nothing to desire,
Beauty of the moment is upon me.

Bliss of ruby red wine,
Slightly oaky,
Smoothly glides from glass to throat.

Even if days are dark and gloomy,
The light in our hearts
Is forever Summer.

A round table with students
Beaming essence
Alive with wine and higher centers.

The large quiet space
After everyone has gone home,
Is a good place to calmly reflect.

Reaching for the highest
Rung of the ladder,
The view is always worth it.

Although it is imprecise
To evaluate one's own progress,
We trust in outside mentors.

Garlands of roses fill the air
With blissful perfume,
Decorating for a festival of love.

The hallway is strewn with petals;
Balloons and streamers greet
Joyous revelers that enter by twos.

Birthday, anniversary, wedding,
A love celebration
Always befits the winery crew.

Words can be powerful
Expressions of love, deep insights,
But nothing like direct experience.

Here and now
Contain everything we need
To be outside of time and space.

Gracious and waiting,
The empty space prepared
For the grand entrance.

The clarity that wine holds
When you lift the glass to toast
Beautifully says it all.

Listening to the pleasant hum
Of spirited winery workers
On the assembly line.

Bottles move along,
Each one representing
A labor of commitment and love.

Deeply penetrating verifications
Support the efforts that bring
Rich California wines to completion.

We dance and sing on level one,
Celebrating our love of wine
And each other.

The rain comes
As Summer fades,
Inward-looking faces count blessings.

A window giving view of the lake
Fills the curtain with fresh breeze,
A new breath of a new day.

The door opens
Bringing in multicolored leaves
With fresh-faced students.

A simple touch
From one hand to the next,
Says everything that has gone before.

Aging in barrels,
Being topped off,
Wine settles in for a long slumber.

Fresh from the tank
Effervescent white wine
Is so strong, it curls your toes.

The cool winery begs
Hot tea to warm cold hands
And soothe tired dispositions.

Winery cats
Keep the rodent population
At a minimum.

With a sweep of her hair
Tucked into a long tail;
Best to keep it away from machinery.

Friends gather to share food,
Wine, and fun,
Always a celebration of love.

Working in silence,
Inner space expanding,
Light of other worlds my guide.

Opening the door to the outside –
Shocking delight!
Rainfall has become snowflakes.

Stars shine down on the
Winery hilltop
Just the same as everywhere else.

But the Milky Way
Pours its blessings
Into the winery tanks every night.

Dancing sprites
With rainbow wings
Layer stardust over the barrels.

If you don't believe me,
I don't blame you,
I've been touched by angels.

In the clear-eyed morning
The process seems ordinary again,
Until we share the product.

Pure light, pure love, pure wine,
A trio in perfect harmony,
With this spectacular day.

Lift your glass to toast
Chardonnay extraordinaire,
A wine of noble bearing.

Learning as a lifelong practice
Opens channels forged in childhood,
Pathways to vivid essence presence.

Hail! to all who labor
In the name of Love,
Gifted a dome of Uncreated Light.

Pure silence reigns
In the inner world
Of all who love presence.

A hawk, white smoke,
Good omens
Of a lost love's presence.

Blow the trumpet
For a good friend's
Departure.

Aching joints can be difficult,
But flexibility of mind and heart
Much more important.

Our lives swim in the ether
Of conscious love,
Affecting higher possibilities.

Samples are tested and retested,
The winemaking science
Is an exacting art form.

Alchemy of transformation,
Water to wine, stone to gold,
Inner life to shining silence.

The night is long
On the winery knoll,
Bats have their way with the moon.

Mind-melting cheese
Goes deliciously with
Our beautiful beverage.

Moving through the inner chambers
Of the winery's heart,
Coming face to face with my Self.

Nights are cold now,
Extra blankets and wood stove fire
Warm extremities.

Lovely ambience,
Evenings of night-blooming jasmine,
Red wine, and You.

Painting the walls,
Polishing the floors,
Maintenance is continuous.

Mistakes are made,
Corrections follow,
Learning continues.

We love,
We are loved,
The very air loves us.

From planting, growing,
Harvesting, distilling,
Wine of understanding is born.

While the raw material of our
Budding souls
Grows into radiant being.

Life, death, rebirth,
Words on a page,
Living breath reads.

Like a testament
To the rocky ground,
The winery rises up before me.

Ritual sounds better than habit,
But only real
With true intention.

Wild and edgy,
Tipsy and ecstatic;
Upright challenged.

New insights swallowed
Into night revelries,
Crazy good moments.

No inner critique
To hinder
Soaring states of essence joy.

Divine visions fade,
Hangover approaches as
Ground comes closer.

Through all,
Unfaltering light
Penetrates my being.

The ascending road
To the winery
Lined with Italian cypress.

Between these green pillars
The lake and Theatron
Are visible.

Vineyard bells signal
Days beginning and end,
Reassuring sound from afar.

Whirling like a dervish,
Locked into a swimming embrace,
Abundant state of grace ensues.

One drop from the forgotten
Wine cup
Leaks to the winery floor.

Earth blood
Seeps back into its source
Cycle complete.

Divinely inspired
Artistry flows through
Open hearts and minds.

We grew along with vines,
We ripened along with grapes,
We were distilled along with wine.

Raking branches filter
Autumn breezes,
Purifying air that is our breath.

Finished bottles
With "Gold Winner" stickers,
My heart leaps to behold.

Coyotes howling in the distance,
Winery dogs chiming in,
Songs of animal essence.

Hierarchy of living beings
Depends upon intelligence,
Not brute force.

Great and small
We are alike,
Born of earth and stars.

Listening to the echoes
Of footsteps on the hard floor,
Marveling at the size of this space.

What stories can be told
In and around this place,
But most of all, the magnificent wine.

Low flying helicopter
Rumbles overhead,
Vertical space suddenly recognized.

Holding inner work
Before my hands and eyes,
My heart bursting with joy.

Love painted the sky
With every color I can see,
And many that I can't.

If nothing concerning us
Is arbitrary,
Even my sleep is calculated.

Like purring cats,
The humming machines
Accompany our efforts.

Life is long or short
Depending on your point of view,
Depth of experience stretches time.

Quiet night,
Walking through empty vines,
Going home until tomorrow.

My whole identity wrapped around
Who everyone thinks I am.
What if they forget? What if I do?

Those with wings will not forget me,
Even if I do.
More love is given than I can hold.

We are attracted to what sings to us,
Invisible realms call for connection;
Muse, fate, angel, guide, higher Self.

All dissolves in divine light;
Bowing in gratitude for supreme gift,
Pure, empty, enlightened heart.

Musical sounds drift in and out
Of deserted halls and stairways,
Remnants of past artistry.

Life takes its toll,
To reside in the holy place,
At times, is most difficult.

The view from the hilltop is grand,
The winery surrounded by hills,
With circular rows of grape vines.

Vivid images invade my memory,
Future and past
Fade in the blaze of this moment.

Even the most meager job
Holds bright promise,
In the cascading light from above.

Sleep makes its bargain
With us invisibly,
The light wonderfully graces us.

Love and light from above
Making all possibilities
Fruitful and divine.

A dance is held to celebrate
End of season abundance,
And beginning of hibernation.

A bright and sunny morning
Greets us on our way to breakfast,
All applaud our closest star.

Working together
Bonds have been forged,
Friendships for a lifetime.

The rains have come,
Inaudible inside this vault,
Outside a barrel is full to the brim.

Rinsed clean,
The winery knoll,
Refreshed and functioning.

Light, the conductor of good tidings,
Sings immortality
To those who listen.

I dreamed I was ascending
High up into the stratosphere,
Grape clusters were falling like rain.

The world is large,
My bubble is small,
But the walls are transparently clear.

It is the best privilege
To be able to greet each other
Daily with love in our hearts.

The doors of my heart
Are flung wide,
Shining forth all that was gifted.

Cubes and spheres,
Geometry of divine laws,
Pointing the way home.

Sweetest light
Pierces darkest crevice,
Honeyed fruit nectar discovered.

Flowers in their hair,
Small girls spread petals
Beneath bridal feet.

Marriage, birth, death,
Milestones continue,
Here, like everywhere.

Full bottles, empty vineyard,
Abundance of magical
Possibilities ahead.

Wine, the special ingredient
That transforms this moment
Into blissful remembrance.

Madness of the gods
Descends to our brows,
Inviting all to perceive divine reality.

Relax unnecessary tension,
Move with aware intention,
Open to the dance of love.

The bluest sky embraces
Winery knoll, ponds,
Surrounding hills and valleys.

The walk through the vines
Draws workers
To a shared meal.

Invisibly the process has endured,
Angelic help
Has ensured success.

Watching bubbles rise in my glass,
Marveling at how
That which is lightest ascends.

Another day of pouring
Superb vintages
From our vaulted storage.

Pure heart and mind
Reveal
One's true self.

Heartstrings
Stretch around the world,
Connecting loving students.

Loving our wines,
Loving each other,
We love our true selves.

Things move in and out
Of our lives,
Only one true thing remains.

Garlands of roses
Wind around support poles of
Billowing white tents.

The festival is on,
Good wine, good food,
On a clear bright day.

We are all winners,
Before the contest
Even begins.

Shafts of sunlight
Stripe the floor,
Lowly dust specks elevated.

Winemaking can be quirky,
From wearing funny hats
To somersaults in midair.

To be a good winemaker
A special palate
Is a necessity.

After the storm,
Large branches on winery road
Force slower ascent.

Tranquil and deep
The waters
Of pure light.

Wishing won't cut it,
Effort is necessary
Until spirit infused.

Suffering needlessly,
Opens inner doors
To unwelcome places.

If the ruling faculty
Is in place,
Harmony can follow.

All great endeavors
Require priority of submission
To the highest perspective.

All things considered,
Our students, not the wines,
Have gained the most.

The struggle is mostly imaginary,
It takes only one step,
Outside sleep.

In the light
It is abundantly clear,
The necessity for presence.

Each of us adds
A personal view
To the spectacular whole.

The years bear down,
Movements slower,
Hearts still take flight.

Bathing in the fresh light
A new day has begun,
Drop old habits and stride forward.

No matter where you are on Earth,
Inner work is always there
And always the same.

For the limited time we
Experience Earth,
Birth and death are the framework.

Missing a friend
Who no longer shares the planet
Is a painful state to transform.

Change and being consistent
Are not opposites.
Change happens, we are consistent.

The French bells are ringing,
A new era has started,
Light strands have united.

A small cat departing,
Can leave a large hole
In one's heart.

Floods of tears
Won't change
A speck of fate.

Bright sun
Cannot dispel
Painful heart woes.

A hearty glass of wine,
Good friends,
Make a great difference.

Be joyous,
Celebrate your blessings,
Strive for acceptance and love.

Life is for the living,
So live with gusto,
Examining every particle.

The invisible
Gives and takes
From the visible.

Nothing is hidden.
It is all
Right before our eyes.

Let love be an ocean
Not a prison,
Open up wide.

The gates of immortality
Require specific
Passage.

The hollow space
Of the winery
Holds many tales.

The trick of
Water into wine,
Is patience.

To reap the benefits
Of a good life,
Requires leaving it.

Genuine trust
Engenders
Its like.

Sharing households
Is advanced work,
For all involved.

To elevate your state,
Look up,
Do a sky dance.

Suffering isn't a waste,
If you are truly accepting
Of the Play.

Flawless hardly ever happens,
But even a blemish
Can trigger refined attention.

It's a red wine night –
Sampling the varietals
Lights a flame in my heart.

Solid walls support
Tipsy steps
To divine madness.

Why don't you know
Who you are?
What stops you?

Death only looks
Dead,
From this side.

When you have arrived,
The only place to go,
Is up.

It is not the place,
It is not the action,
It is not that either.

Move gently,
Love fully,
Generously release all.

We already know enough,
It is time
For letting go of understandings.

Although dark,
The leap is small
From known to unknown.

The drum beat of the Teacher's heart,
Penetrates to the farthest shores
Of our School.

Our gifts are many,
Our gratitude often lacking
Sufficient attention.

Let love be our guide
In all things,
With each other.

A few raindrops
Spatter the winery driveway,
Gray clouds over morning workers.

Sultry afternoons
Sport damp brows;
Winery, cool as ever.

Thunder, lightning!
Oh my,
The bowling gods are at it again.

Strong feelings
Can be fast and gripping,
Source of permission, mysterious.

Prioritizing our inner state
Is a lifelong
Practice.

The pyramid of states,
Should be reversed:
Widest edge at the top – full of light.

Love is shown in many forms,
Better to be present
To them all.

Children, pets, households,
We are responsible for much;
Most of all, our inner state.

Flying high above
The rotating Earth,
All moves together as one.

The art and science
Of winemaking
Produces a joyous result.

Dig a hole in hard earth
And place your sad memories
To rest for as long as it takes.

Fragility of humankind
Is astonishing,
Coupled with stubbornness.

If simple were easy
Problems would be fewer,
Life would be less tangled.

To be graceful and grateful,
Is of a higher order of being,
One seldom attained.

The chiming bells
Reminding of sunny days,
And revels in the night.

Make your steps lighter,
Look up,
Remember you belong to stars.

There is always
Something to say;
Who is there to listen?

Hearing vs. listening,
Is like seeing vs. perceiving:
Someone has to be there.

A jolt awakens
Sleepy heads,
Someone dropped metal trays.

The eternal light dome
Is untouched
By temporal events.

High sugar levels
Make port wine
Delicious.

Here and now,
Is a truly great
Harvest.

Death grows from life,
Seed of change,
Embedded in our fate.

Cosmic influences
Filter down through complex layers,
But reach us nonetheless.

If words could carry my wishes,
Dear reader,
You would receive the best light.

The still center
Of our being
Can determine direction.

When expected,
The backlash from action
Is easier to work with.

At the end of opportunity,
Be grateful,
Be loving.

Patience is an ingredient
Of intelligence,
Without which mistakes occur.

Attention is precious,
Wasted on negativity;
Focus on feeding higher centers.

To understand
The eternal infinite
Leave reason behind.

We are forever
Casting no shadow
As long as it lasts.

Our inner space
Is just as large
As our outer space.

The line between
Seer and seen
Is disappearing.

If this is all Greek
To you,
You are very lucky.

Attend to the highest
In every moment,
The gods rain blessings daily.

Beauty is not an
Adornment,
It is a state of being.

Love quickens
The fuel-less flame,
A beacon to higher centers.

Light upon light
Crowns our every moment,
Even if we cannot perceive it.

All the gods around the world
Have done, will do, are doing
Everything to further our ascent.

Failure is one
Of the repeated
Steps to success.

With hands together,
Heads bowed,
Humbly, we thank Thee.

www.ingramcontent.com/pod-product-compliance
Lightning Source LLC
Chambersburg PA
CBHW031415290426
44110CB00011B/385